Hitchin

IN OLD PHOTOGRAPHS

ALAN FLECK

To Janet & John

From Lorraine & John

Christmas 94

Alan Sutton Publishing Limited
Phoenix Mill · Far Thrupp · Stroud
Gloucestershire

First Published 1994

British Library Cataloguing in Publication Data.
A catalogue record for this book is available from
the British Library.

ISBN 0-7509-0731-2

Typeset in 9/10 Sabon.
Typesetting and origination by
Alan Sutton Publishing Limited.
Printed and bound in Great Britain by
WBC, Bridgend, Mid Glam.

Bustle and activity on the western side of Market Place, *c.* 1902. The stalls in the foreground seem to specialize in clothing, judging by the clothes and fabrics spread over them, while those a little further away to the left contain hats.

Contents

Introduction   5

Acknowledgements   6

1. Animals   7

2. Wheat and Grain   15

3. Pubs   21

4. Shops and Shopping   27

5. Getting About   41

6. Not the Happiest Days . . .   55

7. Entertainments   61

8. Events   71

9. Queen Street   115

This aerial view of Hermitage Road, about 1920, shows the construction of the main shopping and apartment block on the northern side. Ransom's works are clearly visible in the foreground, while there has already been some clearance of buildings fronting Queen Street, south of Portmill Lane. Many buildings still cluster at the south-eastern foot of Windmill Hill – this was Thorpe's Yard.

Introduction

Hitchin has been around for a long time, but the purpose of this book is not to explain how it reached its present shape; rather it is to look at the town during the current century to see how it has changed over that time, preferably using photographs which have not been published before. Some of the changes have been substantial – and those are generally to do with transport or public health in one way or another – while others are subtle. The Queen Street yards have been cleared, the market has moved, a hospital and a flour mill have grown up, outgrown their sites and moved on elsewhere. The post office, rather like a butterfly, has fluttered from Market Place to Brand Street to Hermitage Road, to alight once more in Market Place within a few metres of its birthplace. The motor car has demanded the largest changes – the demise of the wheelwrights, the growth of the mechanics, the car parks and the petrol stations, and now we find ourselves in the later stages of their flight from town centres to the out-of-town supermarkets. Only recently has the pedestrian begun to fight back, though the fruits of his struggle have not been welcomed by all.

At the turn of the century Hitchin was still quite small and tightly integrated. Large imposing houses along Bancroft concealed small yards behind, where families lived and worked in less imposing conditions. Substantial industries flourished close to the river, their work-force rarely living more than ten minutes' walk away. Ransom's still flourishes, but Russell's tannery, the Lucas Brewery and several small maltings have all gone. Small businesses have replaced them in the town centre, while the large employers occupy an area set aside for that purpose, and most of the employees drive to work. It is perhaps ironic that 4 miles away at the beginning of the century Ebenezer Howard was striving to upgrade residential areas and maintain a distributed industrial base in his first Garden City in Letchworth.

These changes are certainly not unique to Hitchin, but they are unique to us as individuals – here a shop gone, there a pub gone, here a new shop, there a new car park. I have tried to pick on changes which will jog the memory and provoke the response 'I'd forgotten that!'

Acknowledgements

All the photographs in this volume come from the substantial collections at Hitchin Museum, notably the Latchmore, *Hertfordshire Express* and *Hertfordshire Pictorial* Collections. The Latchmore Collection numbers some 5,000 prints from a father and son team working in Hitchin from 1863 until 1946. The *Hertfordshire Express* Collection is of comparable size, mainly of modern prints, which rarely date from before 1959, while the *Pictorial* Collection is immense – some 300,000 negatives on glass and film from 1929 until the late 1960s. Together these collections, with many contributions from private individuals and the museum's own documentary work, constitute a magnificent record of Hitchin.

SECTION ONE

Animals

Animals have been sold in Bancroft since at least the fourteenth century and the pens, put up and taken down each market day, were no doubt as much an obstruction then as they were when this photograph was taken in 1893. At this time most of Bancroft was a residential street, and there were complaints from the residents about the noise created when the cattle pens were put up in the early morning on market day.

A view northwards from Moss's Corner, 1903. 'We cannot understand how anyone seeing (and otherwise experiencing) the market as it was last Tuesday – unclean, nauseating, dangerous – could desire its continuance under present conditions.' (*Hertfordshire Express*, 1902.)

Members of the Urban District Council stand by Crabb's Farm in Payne's Park. Government legislation decreed in 1900 that the sale of animals in the street was unhygienic, and was no longer permitted. Hitchin's reaction? 'Except the Church of St Mary . . . we have scarcely any other remnant of the dark and unsanitary yet romantic and picturesque Middle Ages, when men's minds were above smells, and the presence of a few cows . . . did not disturb their equanimity.' (*Hertfordshire Express*, letter to the Editor, 1902.)

Crabb's Farm, 1902. Crabb's Farm off Payne's Park was the site chosen for the new cattle market. In 1902 it still had its farmhouse and a thatched barn against the road.

Payne's Park, 1902–3. Despite the ultimate integrated appearance of the Lairage scheme it was not all one building, as can be seen from this eastward view along Payne's Park. Scaffolding for the new fire station can be seen in the distance.

Payne's Park Lairage and Fire Station, completed in 1903. The completed scheme for Lairage and fire station was an integrated design, with the fire station at the Brand Street end of the site, the pens and sheds behind and a public convenience and a small office unit to the west, flanking the railings to the road. This view was taken by Thomas Latchmore from the rear of his photographic studio in Brand Street, some time after 1903.

The Lairage made provision for the stallage of sheep and other animals, and was used for many years. Seen here around 1908, it looked little different in September 1940 when the *Hertfordshire Pictorial* reported that '3,000 sheep, evacuated in the district, were auctioned at Jackson's Sale Yard'.

The Lairage, 1903. A small cowherd looks on. 'The new cattle market was opened on Tuesday. A fairly large number of sheep and bullocks was brought in and with the baskets of poultry hitherto shown in High Street, attracted a good many farmers . . . there was no indication that the market would suffer by removal from the streets, but rather the contrary.' (*Hertfordshire Express*, 1903.)

Nightingale Road at the station end, *c.* 1905. The introduction of petrol-powered vehicles did not result in every farmer promptly moving his cattle by vehicle, just as the existence of the railway did not immediately cause factories to be built beside it. Cattle were still driven along the roads for many years to come; other road users just had to take evasive action.

Buyers examining stock, July 1966. Pigs were also sold in the Lairage, but an outbreak of swine vesicular disease in the early 1970s caused the movement of the animals to cease temporarily, and it never resumed.

Other stallage was provided by George Jackson & Co., auctioneers, across Payne's Park in what is now a car park and part of a car sales and repair area. Jackson's reorganized their stallage in 1932, and replaced wooden pens with iron pens made by G.W. King, a local firm. This photograph was taken in 1966.

Mr Smyth introduces the next lot in the sale ring, July 1966. The rise of road transport, and a tendency toward centralization, caused a gradual decline in animal sales generally in Hitchin. Sales on this day were certainly quiet, and all animal sales had ceased here by 1980.

Regular poultry sales were held in the long barn structure in the Lairage, as here in 1966. There were cages inside and out to house the live chickens, ducks and rabbits, but there were occasional escapes: a rabbit made it to the museum and library grounds and lived there for several weeks in 1980!

The Lairage from Payne's Park, 1988. By this time the fate of the Lairage site was sealed. For some time it had done excellent duty as a car park, but now the whole site was to be cleared for a multi-storey car park and a large supermarket. This view looks into the Lairage from Payne's Park, past the little ambulance station that had sprung up quietly in the early 1960s.

SECTION TWO

Wheat and Grain

Around Oughton Head in the 1920s. The invention in America of the reaper-binder meant that the twentieth-century farmworker would experience far less of the labour that befell his ancestors. Though much disliked by the horses that drew it, the machine speeded up the harvesting time, and more grain could be spared the ravages of this uncertain climate.

Loading stooks on a cart, Luton Road, 1950s. The photograph was taken by Eric Blundell, a local farmer and photographic enthusiast. The horse has many advantages over the tractor: it has innate intelligence, and once it has grasped the nature of the activity, and with a short instruction, it can usually be relied upon to carry it out. It can even take a cart home if, for some reason, the driver is unable to do so.

Jack Taplin drives a Fordson with 'Scotty' Marvel on the back at the bottom end of Wymondley Road, *c.* 1938. The invention of the tractor has been described as one of the greatest of all social innovations for the farm labourer, as it meant, among other things, that he could drive home for lunch. Its designed-in flexibility, both as a tractive effort for ploughing or pulling wagons and as a source of rotational power to drive other equipment by belt drive or direct shaft, meant there was little it could not do. And unlike a horse, it did not play hard to get in the morning.

Captain S.M.E. Fairman, Chief Constable of Hertfordshire, on his working holiday in 1943. The arrival of the combine harvester speeded up the harvesting process yet further by cutting, threshing and winnowing on the move.

Bowman's Mill, Nightingale Road, 1904. Once sold, the wheat could travel in several directions. One course was to Bowman's Mill. While the Corn Exchange had been built very soon after the arrival of the railway in the town, Bowman's Mill was not built until some five decades had passed. It is not clear whether this was from uncertainty about the benefits of rail for freight transport, or whether the land simply was not available. Initially the mill was powered by steam.

Bowman's Mill, 1985. By the mid-1980s Bowman's had expanded their business to the limits of the site, and the decision was taken to leave Cambridge Road and move to Ickleford. By this time the building itself had grown, and only a fragment of the original structure remained visible.

Wratten maltings, Hitchin's last functioning malting, on Wratten Road, off Tilehouse Street, *c.* 1930. While wheat is used for culinary purposes, barley is used for brewing, and Hitchin had once sported many maltings, where the grain was spread out under controlled environmental conditions to germinate. As time went on the number of local breweries declined, and the arrival of the railway meant that much barley could be exported, particularly to the many breweries around the River Trent.

Wratten Road shortly before the whole site was cleared in the early 1960s. The site of the Wratten is now occupied by bank offices. The malting had ceased to operate many years earlier, and the yard had been used for the storage of building equipment by a local building company.

Children at work on the lavender harvest, 1943. Wheat and barley were of course not the only plants grown around Hitchin. Hitchin was known world-wide for Perks & Llewellyn's lavender products, and this photograph, which appeared in the *Comet*, was probably included as a morale booster – life is proceeding as normal, despite the war. The paper referred as little as possible to military events.

Pea picking in Crosspath Field in the 1950s. Other crops were even more labour-intensive than lavender, and peas were a crop where care was necessary. Large parties would go out into the field, and, judging by this group, the occasions were treated almost as social events. One small boy still has his school cap on.

SECTION THREE

Pubs

The Bull's Head, Tilehouse Street, 1902. A private house since 1916, the Bull's Head was first recorded as a pub in 1757, when it was sold to William Lucas for £150. The 1841 census recorded that it housed James Reynolds, his wife and their seven children, and Michael Ansell, his wife and their six children. Here it is decorated for the celebrations of the coronation of Edward VII.

High Street pubs, 1899. For many years the High Street had pubs in three adjacent buildings – the Three Horseshoes (left), the White Horse (centre) and the Black Horse. Presumably the names refer back to earlier times when part of the street was used for horse-dealing. The White Horse closed shortly after 1906, and the other two in 1958.

The Cock Hotel, 1930. By the 1930s there was marked advantage to be gained from a High Street site; the town was ready to welcome chain stores, and Woolworths wanted to move in. To make way for the new store approximately two-thirds of the Cock Hotel was demolished, leaving the building as we know it today – truncated to two bays, one with two storeys, the other with three. Perks & Llewellyn's, next door on the right, was demolished in 1964, and Woolworths then moved on to that site.

The Angel Vaults, seen here in 1956, was constructed at least as early as 1450. Henry VIII is said to have stayed at the pub at one time, escaping from a fire there clad only in his night-shirt. Owned in 1787 by William Lucas of the local brewing family, it was a Lucas tied house by 1817, and was bought by McMullens in 1912.

The Horse & Jockey, *c.* 1910. This was the most recent pub to disappear in Hitchin, demolished in 1990. It was built by Joseph Margetts Pierson, a banker, shortly before 1844. The Inspector of Public Nuisances noted, in slight puzzlement, in 1900: 'During heavy storms sewage is headed up in the back yard of this inn. I think something must be wrong with the private sewer.' Unusually, a substantial part of the pub was built of clunch or chalk block, rather than brick.

A delightfully clear view of shops in Market Place in 1912, especially of the Red Cow, to the right of the telegraph pole. Built in 1676, the pub was licensed in 1912 to Joseph Slaney, who had lived there since 1886. However, he died the year he became licensee, and his wife succeeded him until 1929. In 1961 it became an off-licence, run by Threshers.

The Adam and Eve, 1933. In the mid-nineteenth century Hitchin had one pub for every fifty inhabitants, be they man, woman or child. That ratio has dropped since then; the population has risen and the number of pubs has declined. Many of the pubs have themselves changed quite radically. The Adam and Eve was a public house in Bancroft in 1672 when Sarah Adams obtained a licence for James Rogers, an Independent, to preach there – a strangely appropriate function for a pub of this name! By 1933 it had long been a brick house with a mansard roof, and that side of Bancroft was known as The Bank because of its raised pavement.

The Cart Horse and Tradesmen Parade in progress, passing the Rose and Crown on Bank Holiday Monday, 7 August 1899. The early life of the Rose and Crown is obscure. There was a pub with that name in Hitchin, but it is not clear from existing records whether it was this building in Market Place or another, in Sun Street. By 1720 this building was let by Joseph Marsom, its rent paying for the poor boys of Hitchin to be apprenticed to Freemen of the City of London. In 1818 it was leased to the brewer Henry Crabb, and described in 1839 as 'an ancient edifice requiring constant repair'. It was finally demolished in 1935 and the present building erected in its place.

The demolition of The Crown and The White Lion at Moss's Corner resulted in a fusion of the two taverns on part of the original site, but the bar was entirely underground. Next door was occupied by Tesco stores. This photograph was taken at the closure of The Crown and Lion in 1979.

The Waggon and Horses, photographed in 1981, was to last a little longer than the Crown and Lion. Built as one of a group of four cottages in the late eighteenth century, it passed through the hands of Marshall's Brewery, Pryor's, Simpson's, and finally Greene King before closing in 1972. It was demolished some nine years later.

SECTION FOUR
Shops and Shopping

Market Place, *c.* 1893. Hitchin market-place is a clear space, quite deliberately left to permit trading to take place in the street. Our (relatively) modern naming of Sun Street, Bucklersbury, Churchyard and High Street obscures the fact that all these streets were once one, stretching from Bancroft to Tilehouse Street. Trading was extensive and covered the greater part of that street; sheep, pigs and cattle were sold from the northern end, while the daily necessities of fruit, vegetables, hardware and textiles were on offer in Market Place itself.

Rennie's Bible and book stall, *c.* 1900. James Rennie sold religious tracts and moral tales from a stall typical of those from centuries gone by: a canvas tilt spread over un-worked timber supports, with goods displayed on boards over trestles. John Beaver (who ran the post office when it was in Market Place) stands on the left, E.C. Wilmott in the shade of the awning, and James Rennie on the right.

Perks & Llewellyn's window, High Street, 1900. Shop window-dressing early this century seems to have had much more to do with effects of mass, repetition and colour than with subtlety. Wright's Coal Tar products are the only brand on display in the window, having virtually obscured the coloured carboys which were the pharmacists' trademark. Violet Lewis, Perks's last pharmacist, remarked: 'We took the carboys out of the window in 1939. I found that the yellow one was mostly picric acid (an explosive), and the blue was copper sulphate in acid – it ate through the bucket I used to bale it out!'

Jackson's shop, Market Place, 1902. Jackson's shop was a typical development of a private house, with very little concession to the actual business of shop display – some plate glass windows and a small bay window on the High Street side were all that were needed. Beside it, in the High Street, was a private house that seems not to have become a shop until around 1930, when it became David Greig's, the grocer's.

Brand Street post office, 1912. The post office had long been something of a movable feast in Hitchin, beginning life in what is now Merrick's shop at the Market Place end of High Street, and then moving to the eastern half of what is now Briggs's shoe shop. In 1903 a new post office was purpose-built in Brand Street. The staff were numerous, and this formal portrait comprises the postmaster, the overseer, male and female sorting clerks and telegraphists, telephonists, town postmen, rural postmen, and messenger boys.

Moss's Corner, 1905. Most shops were in Market Place and the High Street, but over the years some have crept insidiously down Bancroft. Moss's shop, which gave Moss's Corner its name, took over the Old Trooper pub; next door on the left stood the vicarage, then The Crown, and The Lion (at this time two separate pubs). In 1901 Moss's shop was extensively remodelled and an extra floor was inserted.

The Christmas display at Odie & Marshall's, Brand Street, 1904. Odie & Marshall's was at the bottom end of Brand Street from 1904 until 1929, selling haberdashery and small items of clothing.

Sun Street, suddenly flooded in 1912. Shops in Sun Street dealt in more mundane things than those in Market Place. Williams and Son were hardware merchants selling tin wares, traveller's trunks, hat boxes, and even a rose pergola outside their shop. Bridge Street and the southern end of Sun Street were subject to sudden inundations after heavy rain for many years, the problem only being solved by additional drainage in the 1980s.

The staff of Brooker's, Sun Street, in the 1920s. Tom Brooker came to Hitchin in 1876, opened a shop (initially in Walsworth Road and still there today, split into multiple single-storey units), and later took over Williams and Son's shop in Sun Street. The business eventually moved further up Sun Street, and expanded there both sideways and backwards into Exchange Yard.

A margarine queue snakes around the edge of Market Place, 1915. There was some rationing of dairy produce during the First World War and butter and margarine were not always in plentiful supply. Just to the right of the tall telegraph pole stands the Red Cow, a pub since the seventeenth century, and to the right of Halsey's, the Rose and Crown.

On the south side of Market Place the International Tea Company was to succeed Melia's Teas at the turn of the century. The sides of mild-cured bacon flanking the shop, and the advertisements for butters and margarines in the left-hand bay window, indicate that they clearly did not specialize in tea alone.

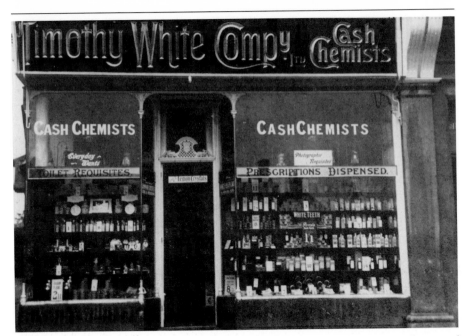

Timothy White's, cash chemists, who moved to the Corn Exchange in 1915. The use of town centre properties by the retail trade resembles a slow and stately game of tag. If a property falls vacant, another trader will move to occupy it, seeing some advantage in doing so – once a shop, always a shop.

Maison Gerard, 1920. Across the square from White's, this shop was another legacy of the war. Like many others, Gerard Ceunis had fled his native Belgium at the beginning of the war, and had settled in north Hertfordshire. In Market Place he founded a ladies' outfitter's shop. A painter of considerable ability, he exhibited in many well-known galleries in London, and a representative collection of his works is held by local museums. This corner of the square had long had a bias towards the sale of clothing: the timber-framed buildings on the right housed both a milliner and a tailor.

Hitchin market-place, 1929. The wooden market stalls remained in use for a long time, obviously well suited to their task and easy to put up and take down. All around, people go about their business, showing very little regard for the passing traffic. Right of centre stands the Midland Bank, erected here in 1926, then as now adjoining Briggs's shoe shop. At night – for market day extended well after dark – the market stalls were lit by paraffin lamps.

The butcher of Doling & Procter's shop in Bucklersbury stands proudly in front of his display window, decked with promotional signs and conversational pigs' heads, 1931. In more leisurely days there was time to participate in competitions such as this, the Empire Window-Dressing Competition.

The International Stores at Bucklersbury, decorated for the coronation in 1937. Freeman, Hardy & Willis's awning hangs out on the right, next is Eastman's the butcher's, then Waldock & Sons, gentlemen's outfitter's. Ladders lean against the Red Lion, a pub which had been displaced from Market Place by the construction of the Corn Exchange in 1853.

The High Street in 1938, with Woolworths installed between Barclays Bank and the Cock Hotel. While it could be argued that all early Woolworths stores look the same, the style, with its classical overtones, blends in well with the Italianate features of the bank next door.

Hitchin's first supermarket opened in 1949 in Nightingale Road. The new style of shopping was so alien it had to be explained. 'Briefly speaking, the customer takes a wire basket at the entrance, selects the goods she [she!] wants . . . and pays at the checkout. Rationing makes complete self-service an impossibility. . . .' (*Hertfordshire Pictorial*, 31.8.49.)

The Croft in Bancroft was one of the last buildings to change from private house to shop. Here in 1955 it still stands much as it had been since 1859, when the banker Charles Prime had combined two late medieval cottages into one Gothic-revival town house. In 1955 it was occupied by Charles and Hubert Moss. Their departure allowed Bancroft to complete its change from an almost exclusively residential street (at the beginning of the twentieth century) to a street completely dedicated to shopping.

The Book House, seen here about 1964, was obviously a bookshop and general stationer's, while Shilcock's, built on the site of the Six Bells pub in 1868, still displayed its fine metal lettering. Just off the left edge of the picture was the Home & Colonial Stores, for all your grocery needs.

Woolworths assistants re-stock the gondolas in 1965. While the *Pictorial* may have felt it necessary to explain how you shop in a supermarket, its readers took up the new style with some relish. Woolworths new store in the High Street was in the new style from day one.

The main framework of the new market buildings takes shape beside Biggin Lane in July 1972. The view is westward along Churchyard Walk past Warner's Almshouses on the extreme right.

The Croft, 1973. The Croft was demolished in the 1960s and rebuilt as a pastiche of its former self, with its interior spaces reorganized for modern use. In 1973 it contained an outfitter's, Loyds, selling electrical goods such as refrigerators, televisions and radios, and Sketchley's, the dry-cleaner's.

Safeways under construction on Bancroft, 1974. After the old Waters' site was cleared, the plot remained vacant for a while. The object of the new structure may have been to provide a visual 'full-stop' at the end of Hermitage Road, but the graceless structure now on that site is used as a model to architecture students of how not to marry the new with the old.

Safeways, Bedford Road, 1989. Early in 1989 work began on the Lairage site, which had been used as a car park for several years. The 1929 Infirmary wings were demolished and a substantial steel structure arose, soon to become a large superstore and a multi-storey car park. The nurses' home at the northern tip of the triangular site was later demolished.

SECTION FIVE

Getting About

Flanders' façade, 1902. Flanders sold bicycles, carriages and, in time, motor car bodies. In the early days cars were quite literally horseless carriages, and the skill of the carriage-builder was exercised on the motor car just as if it were a horse-drawn vehicle temporarily missing the horse. The car here, probably a Daimler, has a passenger compartment remarkably similar to that of the governess-carts often seen around the town at this time. Nose to nose as if in a duel, the motor car was the ultimate winner.

Fred Carling, local newspaper owner, and his wife, Grace, and elder son, Alan. The motor car was initially only for the well-to-do, who could afford to order the bodywork on a chassis provided by the car-maker. Mrs Carling (as Grace Plowman) was one of the first intake of pupils at Hitchin Girls' Grammar School, and one of the first girls from the school to get a degree, at Owen's College, Manchester.

The Gainsford motor-trike, driven by the Revd G. Bernard Gainsford, with his wife as passenger. For those for whom the motor car was too expensive, or viewed as an indulgence, there were some alternatives, such as this delightful petrol tricycle.

A motley array of vehicles parked outside the Corn Exchange during the 1906 election campaign, won by Mr Miller. It is all too tempting to see the car as a problem and to forget that the horse brought problems too – parking the car was initially just as random an activity as parking the horse and cart. By 1906 Flanders had left the northern part of their shop, which was next occupied by the International Stores, the latter maintaining a presence in the town centre until the mid-1970s.

The charabanc was to prove as popular a mode of group transport as the minibus is today. Here in 1913 Mr Burroughs stands ready to drive (from second left) 'Peggy' Watson, Len Foster, Joe Seymour, Joe Williams, Mr Parson and Ernie Gower on a trip, starting from the Coopers' Arms in Tilehouse Street.

Hermitage Road, 1923. The motor omnibus was an effective mode of regular transport, though not without its drawbacks – passengers occasionally had to get out and push up steep hills. Little changed here since its creation in 1874, Hermitage Road served as a useful bus-stop.

Delivery men from Wallace's Bancroft Dairy stand outside the dairy itself at the northern end of Bancroft. For daily delivery work the horse or pony was still unbeatable.

For the sweet manufacturers Garratt & Cannon, whose works were in Bancroft until 1932, the light motor lorry was a godsend for their delivery work. Creaseys of Knebworth were a major local vehicle body-builder, and Lacre of Letchworth made both car and lorry chassis in Letchworth, one of the larger industries of the early Garden City.

For regular heavy work the steam lorry was unbeatable, though obviously it needed copious supplies of fuel and water. It was a favourite of brewers because of its considerable capacity. Locally both Pryor Reid and the Lucas brewery used steam lorries.

A traction engine prepares to deliver a new boiler to Russell's tannery, by Woodside, in the 1920s. For occasional really tough work you couldn't beat a traction engine, which was specifically designed for pulling heavy loads. Though the traction engine was originally designed for ploughing – winching a multiple plough across flattish fields – it was later to sprout all manner of strange excrescences including belt drives, and dynamos for showmen's displays.

The town centre, seen here in 1926, was an informal meeting-place and a good point from which to start a trip. While the charabancs wait for their patrons outside the Playhouse Cinema, their drivers stand and chat. The street lamp on the right had a gas fitting during the First World War, from which gas-powered vehicles could replenish their gas-tanks.

Later on, concessions to the motor car appeared. This is the roundabout at the northern end of Bancroft in April 1937, planted in red, white and blue flowers to mark the coronation of George VI. Beyond is the Bancroft Recreation Ground and on the left the gas-holder of the Tottenham and District Company's Gasworks at Starlings Bridge.

Market Place in the early 1960s. Parking was an increasing problem. Until now the main route through was diagonally from High Street to Sun Street, and the parking laid out in 1930 had been made to fit in with this. However, it is difficult to fit cars into a triangular car park: those in the middle find it hard to get out.

The first day of traffic wardens in Hitchin, 4 August 1966. By now two solutions had been devised. The first was to provide parking spaces in ordered rows, with the traffic circulating around them, and the second was to provide traffic wardens to discourage transgression.

Congestion at Moss's Corner, 1963. There were difficulties elsewhere too. This bottleneck, thought to be caused largely by taxis, was in front of the White Lion and the Crown.

Saunders's garage, Queen Street, 1963. Saunders's garage in Queen Street incorporated a petrol station. Over the last few decades petrol stations have generally moved out of town centres. Brand Street, Hermitage Road and Bridge Street all had a petrol pump at one time, but the profit margin on petrol today does not cover the high commercial rents town centre sites attract. Nor, of course, is there always adequate space to accommodate the traffic. Petrol stations have therefore moved away from town centres, and out-of-town supermarkets have added petrol to their list of product lines.

Lower Tilehouse Street, August 1981. Hitchin's traffic load soon began to annoy the inhabitants, and as early as 1933 a bypass was mooted. Various plans were aired, but only in the 1970s did there appear to be any chance of it coming to pass. Buildings in Tilehouse were suffering actual damage as some were struck by passing lorries, and congestion was regular.

Although presumably there had been some consideration of the bypass by the Ministry, the inhabitants began to grow more vocal, and posters started to appear. This one, in Tilehouse Street, was photographed in 1977.

The route finally agreed for the bypass required the demolition of two small cottages at the Tilehouse Street–Old Park Road junction. At one time the cottage on the right, seen here in the late 1970s, had been a pub by the name of the Swan with Two Necks, the necks being a mis-read for nicks (in the beak), by which swans were identified.

The view westwards from the Moorhens Bridge at the southern end of the new road, called Priory Way and classified now as a relief road rather than a bypass, in 1986. Four years after completion the scars have almost healed: eight years later, it seems strangely devoid of vegetation.

The railway was extremely labour-intensive, and this staff photograph at the station in 1906 indicates just how many people were needed at that time to maintain the system. This vast array includes ticket collectors, telegraphists, clerks and porters. There are one or two outsiders here, though; second from the left in the fourth row back, with his impressive beard, stands James Rennie, who may have sold religious tracts at the station as well as in Market Place.

Hitchin station, seen here in 1974, saw two small changes that have probably slipped most memories. Though by no means an original feature – although I have yet to find any record of its arrival – the porte-cochère was a help to those who arrived at the station by road in poor weather. Plans to reorganize the car parking, and no doubt curb inexorably rising maintenance costs, saw the dismantling of the great iron canopy in December 1974.

Hitchin station, 1976. For many years drivers of the cabs, whether petrol or horse-powered, had taken refuge in a cosy, purpose-built structure. By 1976 it had seen better days and was removed. It still exists in private hands.

Benslow Bridge – the moment of detonation late in the night of 20 February 1975. The 1980s saw the introduction of overhead catenary wiring as a move towards a purely electric mainline system. Apart from the enormous task of wiring up the mainline and all the attendant sidings and sheds, much effort had to be spent on ensuring greater clearance for cabling.

SECTION SIX

Not the Happiest Days . . .

The Old Free School, Tilehouse Street, 1949. The Old Free School building was constructed around 1650, mostly of brick. The school had been founded in 1639 by John Mattock (who may be the 'M' on shields around the south porch of St Mary's) but there was always dispute over what should be taught – just enough to enable a tradesman to survive, or Greek and Latin too. The squabble was never resolved until the last master, John Sugars, retired in 1876 through ill health, and the Trustees closed the school. It was to reopen elsewhere thirteen years later as Hitchin Boys' Grammar School. The building here was demolished in 1949 when the road was widened.

Teacher Louisa Allen stands with her charges, Girls Class 6, at St Saviour's School, Radcliffe Road, *c.* 1910. St Saviour's church had been built in 1865, and the school had been built across the road in 1868 to house, after enlargement in 1893, 250 juniors and 150 infants. By 1926 it was taking only girls at junior level and infants. There was also a St Saviour's Orphanage School, which took twenty-four girls.

Class 4a sit in the corner of the great Lancasterian hall of the British School in Queen Street, 1926. At the back stand Mr Corbett, the headmaster, and Captain Hill. Front row, left to right: Tom Maddison, J. Bonfield, Joe Turner, 'Lardy' Westwood, ? Ludford, Freddie Harrold and Joe Bailey. Mr Corbett was regarded by many of the boys as neither fair nor merciful.

Miss Dawson's class at Queen Street, Christmas 1933, lined up on the steps outside the cavernous Lancasterian hall. Back row, left to right: Raymond Lindford, Peter Guthrie, Sheila Brennan, Bruce Lusk, John Godfrey, -?-, Alec Worbey. Second row: -?-, Eric Turner, Fred Barrow, Ernie Richards, Eric Foster, Ronald Ludford. Third row: Isobel Cherry, Peter Hudson, -?-, Jessie Tuffield, -?-, John Darker. Front row: George Brown, Kenneth Hunt, Mavis ?, -?-, Albert Tasker, Audrey Handscombe, Beryl Ludford, Betty Williams.

St Mary's School was built in 1854 at a cost of £4,020, and was externally decorated in diaper-work patterns popular at the time – there are further examples at St Saviour's in Radcliffe Road.

A formal portrait of St Mary's School, winner of the North and East Herts. Musical Festival Sight-Singing Competition for Mixed Voices in 1935.

The Governors of Hitchin Boys' Grammar School attending Speech Day in 1939. At this stage the war had not greatly affected the life of the school, and the routine had continued much as usual. The Governors, who presided at the Speech Day, were, left to right: Miss E. Seebohm, Mr T.E. Jones (the headmaster), Dame Margaret Tuke, Mrs Hugh Seebohm, Mr Hugh Seebohm, Mr G.W. Russell, and Mr C.J. Widdows.

The first headmistress of Hitchin Girls' School was Miss Gosnell, pictured here in 1908, clad in mortar-board and gown in the middle of the front row. The school had been formally opened by the Master of Trinity College, Cambridge, on 25 July. It had moved from 21 Bancroft (almost opposite Hermitage Road), and the move was not popular with all the pupils – 'How far away from the boys!'

Pupils of the Girls' and Boys' Grammar Schools practising Shaffer's method of resuscitation at the new open-air swimming pool on Butts Close, August 1939.

The Old Hale Way School, Bessemer, 1940. Although the school buildings were not quite finished by the beginning of June 1940, the pupils all moved in and set to work, but not quite in the ways one might expect. The boys dug up the quadrangle to plant vegetables, and the girls started making roller-towels and tablecloths for the school.

SECTION SEVEN

Entertainments

The newspaper was an important document at the turn of the century, as the only available means of transmitting accurate records of events other than by word of mouth. Here paper is being unloaded at Carling & Co.'s printing works in Exchange Yard. The Great Northern Railway had its own fleet of flat wagons, with which it delivered goods from the station to local customers.

Carling's Composing Room, 1906. The printing works must have been a noisy place to work, with the murmur of the men in the composing room, the chatter of the girls in the sewing and packing rooms, the presses spinning along, the clack of the joints in the belt drive and the gentle whooshing of the big gas engine on the ground floor that drove all the machinery.

The town's first public library – there were other subscription libraries – was in Brand Street, an 1860 addition to the old 1840 Town Hall. Here it is being opened by a representative of the County Council, which adopted it in 1928.

Payne's Park public library and museum, 1955. In the 1930s Hubert Moss gave his home, Charnwood, to the town for the purposes of a museum and library. It opened in 1939, having been extensively altered inside and out – the front door originally faced Payne's Park, for example. A town museum had been considered around 1915 but nothing had come of it. The new library building was added to Charnwood in 1965.

Mrs Delme-Radcliffe talks to visitors to the Priory, some time in the early 1920s. The Priory, though the private home of the Delme-Radcliffe family until the 1960s, was always made available for the annual fête and other major occasions. The majority of the festivities surrounding the Duchess of York's opening of the new wing of the Infirmary were held there, as was the gun salute for the 1937 coronation celebration. Mrs Delme-Radcliffe was a devout follower of the current fashions.

Mrs Delme-Radcliffe inspects a scout troop on parade in the Priory grounds in the 1920s.

Hitchin Thespians' production of *Veronique*, 1929. Hitchin has been well served by its dramatic societies for many years; the Thespians staged this production in Hitchin Town Hall.

Participants in the North and East Herts. Music Festival of 1929 pose for the camera in Hitchin Town Hall. There was considerable collaboration – and competition – between schools in various areas before the National Curriculum was invented.

Members of Hitchin Band with their president, Ralph Delme-Radcliffe, after winning the London and Home Counties Band Contest at Highbury, London, on 15 July 1922. Many towns have a band of some kind, but Hitchin Band has always been a good one.

The coffee bar, where a black coffee and marshmallow could be had for 10*d*., became the place to be for the young people of the town and is seen here in 1961. The posters on the counter advertise a Police Dance at the Hermitage Halls, admission 10*s*. 6*d*. including buffet, and more interestingly, lots of jazz, regularly every Monday evening.

Brand Street Town Hall dance band, 1961. On 6 February 1961, in Hitchin's own friendly Town Hall, it was the turn of – and won't you please give a big hand to – the inimitable . . . George Melly!

'Young teenagers let themselves go during a rock 'n roll session.' (*Hertfordshire Pictorial.*) There was always dancing and large firms put on dances for their employees, such as this one at Hitchin Town Hall in January 1958, where members of Kryn & Lahy's staff are enjoying themselves.

The Hermitage Cinema, photographed in 1944, had a short life but a popular one. Capable of seating up to 1,300 patrons, and with twelve dressing-rooms, the Hermitage could have been a major venue in the town, but perhaps the population was too small to support so many cinemas once television had arrived.

The Regal Cinema in Bancroft was built in a more futuristic design than other cinemas in Hitchin, with its flat roofs over curved panels with curved windows. It closed in 1979, after unsuccessful attempts to operate it as a popular music venue. The site was subsequently redeveloped to become Regal Chambers.

Blake's Picturedrome is mentioned elsewhere, but only in its 1911 incarnation as a single-storey structure. Such was the success of its programmes of boxing and theatrical events that it was soon expanded with true cinematic flamboyance – a *ménage à trois* of Roman austerity (ground floor entrance), baroque extravagance (rounded pediment and pilasters), and English delicacy (the bow window). It is seen here in February 1962 after closure.

In 1929 the Council installed a slide on land off Grove Road, an action applauded by many small persons.

For those of a more energetic disposition, there was the Queen Street swimming pool, still a vivid memory for many. Unheated, the choice of which day to go swimming posed a dilemma. Early in the week it was crystal clear – and extremely cold. By the end of the week it was green, but much warmer, heated by the passage of many bodies through it.

Aquasplash class in Hitchin's new indoor swimming pool, which opened in 1991. It now attracts 370,000 visitors each year, rather more than the old Queen Street pool.

SECTION EIGHT

Events

Bucklersbury is gaily decked with bunting in celebration of the relief of Mafeking, 24 May 1900. The relief of the town, besieged in the early stages of the Boer War, was marked by exuberant rejoicing throughout the land, to the extent that 'mafeking' came to mean, for a short time at least, 'extravagant rejoicing'.

It is easy to forget that much of Hitchin is relatively modern, and that generally only the very core of the town is of great antiquity. This view of Nuns Close, looking westwards to Old Park Road, was taken at the turn of the century. At this time Charnwood – now Hitchin Museum – was the only building in the short street. The building at the far left is the sole remaining building today, and that has had its door moved to the northern side.

The New Town Hall, Brand Street, 1900. Mr Jelly had for many years run his tin-smithing business at the top of Brand Street, and hosted meetings of the Hitchin Technical Class there. By the end of the century it became clear that a more substantial public hall was needed, both for public meetings and for dramatic performances, and his land was bought for the purpose.

Mr Jelly's house on Brand Street, 1900, part of the site of the New Town Hall.

The foundations of the New Town Hall being laid by Fosters, the local builders. Designs were drawn up by architect Geoffrey Lucas, a relative of the Quaker brewing family, and E.W. Lucas, and work began.

Completed at a cost of £7,300 – with complaint from one Councillor, who maintained there was no room for future expansion – the New Town Hall opened in 1901. This view was taken by Thomas Latchmore from the comfort of his own premises across the street; as usual there was an official opening, attended by the bicycle troop of the Yeomanry.

Moss's Corner, decorated for the coronation of Edward VII in 1902. The local photographer, Thomas Latchmore, documented the town's celebrations in a complete bound album of prints, including press cuttings of unparalleled enthusiasm. 'For some kind of decoration the inhabitants were prepared by witnessing the erection of the white masts and crossbars, but it was not until the very eve of the coronation that they grasped the completeness and beauty of the scheme. Far into the night willing hands laboured, giving the finishing touches . . . Avenues of Venetian masks, fluttering pennons of scarlet, gleaming crowns . . . ' (*Hertfordshire Express.*)

Mr Parker's house, Bancroft, formerly No. 12 Bancroft, 1902. 'Then there was hurrying with the householders to adorn their houses: wreaths, garlands, flags, Chinese lanterns, thousands of lamps seemed to grow upon the walls, and in an hour such a transformation had been wrought in this quiet country town, that the cyclists rushing through from all corners of the country paused, thinking they had missed their way and fallen into the midst of a Continental "Festa". "We have seen nothing like it elsewhere", they were continually saying.' (*Hertfordshire Express.*)

'Soon after one o'clock the streets began to show signs of greater activity and the crowd assembled at points of vantage. As the constituent parts of the procession arrived in Brand Street they were relegated to their various letters in accordance with a well-arranged plan. Beginning at A, the fountain in Bedford Road, Z was not reached before the Wesleyan Church in Brand Street. . . . The leading car of importance was, appropriately enough, Britannia . . . on the top being seated the familiar figure of Britannia, complete with trident shield and all, from whose helmet at night there shone out three brilliant electric lights.' (*Hertfordshire Express.*)

'The Blue Cross Temperance Brigade were responsible for two cars, both of which were very well done. One represented "Nations of the World", and the other "Sports". The sports car was mounted on a timber waggon, and carried representatives of the cricket club with wickets, & etc., in the front, of the football club with their ball, at the back, and of the gymnastic club, with the parallel bars in the middle.' The Nations of the World car is just visible in the centre, and the Sports car to the right. (*Hertfordshire Express.*)

'The "Peace" car . . . was extremely well conceived. The whole structure was draped with cloth of red white and blue, over which was laid a scarlet carpet. Surmounting the platform appeared a huge globe, upon which was painted a copy of the earth's surface. Upon this stood the Angel of Peace (Miss M. Davis) who looked charming in flowing robes of white, bearing in the one hand a laurel wreath, upon which rested a dove, and in the other a corn covered staff.' (*Hertfordshire Express.*)

Electricity cables being laid in the town centre, across the eastern side of Market Place, in 1906. While gas lighting was still installed in new houses for many years, the more well-to-do were soon able to light their homes by electricity, which was quieter, odour-free, and gave a brighter light. It has been argued that electric light stimulated the rise of the vacuum cleaner, as the dirt could now be seen. . . .

The town's fire brigade aboard the old manual pump, outside the fire station in Payne's Park, 1908.

The opening ceremony for the Windmill Hill water tower, 1909. 'This town is often on the verge of a water famine on account of the inadequacy of the storage tank.' So found a local enquiry in 1906, and three years and £11,000 later, Theodore Ransom, Chairman of the Urban District Council, was able to invite guests to this event. Those on the front row include W.B. Moss (second left), W.O. Times (centre), and William Ransom (second right).

The accession of George V in 1911 was proclaimed from the steps of the New Town Hall in Brand Street by the High Sheriff of the County, Sir Alfred Reynolds, who had motored directly from Hertford after making the proclamation there. The dais party – the Chairman of the Council, Theodore Ransom, and others – then set off for the Priory in an open carriage, passing the Brand Street Methodist chapel, the post office, and Odie & Marshall's haberdashery shop on the way down to the High Street.

The celebrations for George V's coronation were to exceed even those of his predecessor. The procession set off on 22 June 1911 at 11 a.m. from Market Place, and wound its way eventually to Butts Close. At various points along the route cameramen recorded the procession on moving pictures.

The fire brigade was present, as always at such events, driving down Bancroft in their new motor appliance. Behind them came representatives of many other local organizations. 'The railway and ancient and modern post office were both interesting local cars, and the decorated motor cars were delightful floral pictures.' (*Hertfordshire Express.*)

'Ancient Britons and Roman soldiers were the first figures in the historical pageant. There was no opposition to the landing of the Normans; on the contrary, their approach was the signal for applause all along the route. The motor power under the vessel lent a modern touch, and the sun-burnt, sea-hardened warriors made a commanding picture.' (*Hertfordshire Express.*) The motor power was in fact a steam traction engine. Here the Normans, hotly pursued by Kershaw's Hitchin coach, pass Waters's furniture shop, just north of the old police station in Bancroft.

The complete procession gathered at Butts Close, where Frederick A. Delme-Radcliffe led the assembled crowds in three rousing cheers for his majesty, and then saluted. Before him stands the cinematographer, steadily winding the handle of his camera.

Within a few days Blake's Picturedrome in Ickleford Road, still dressed overall in celebratory bunting, was showing the results of the cameramen's efforts: the posters advertise showings of 'The Coronation Procession'. Eighty years later a copy of that film is still treasured by Hitchin Museum.

While motor vehicles had featured in the coronation processions, the new technology of the petrol engine had also quickly been applied to the aeroplane, itself only a decade old. Reliability was not a feature of the early petrol engine: Captain Hamilton and Lt. Wyness Stuart were killed when a valve-rod broke in their engine near Graveley in September 1912. The two men were buried with full military honours. Here their funeral cortège approaches Hitchin station.

Frederick Peter Delme-Radcliffe addresses a recruiting meeting in Market Place early in 1915. When the First World War began such meetings were held all over the country. Representatives of the military occupy the cars on the left, while the populace listen, under a sea of straw hats and a few bonnets.

Rapidly the war was to swing from a jingoistic merry-go-round of recruiting meetings to a horrific slogging match of carnage in France and Belgium. As the stalemate continued and individual attacks cost tens of thousands of lives, ever more men were needed. Here, in 1915, Richard Lewis holds a recruiting poster in Perks & Llewellyn's Yard off the High Street: 'We want more men. Another half million needed. Join today.'

For the men who did come back, there was rest and recreation in the Old Town Hall in Brand Street, still very much a social venue. This canteen was operated by the YMCA in 1915.

Peace celebrations, like coronations, were marked by processions. Here in Sun Street on 19 July 1919 elements of the procession gather. The procession began at 7.30 p.m. headed by the Town Band, and the route went along Old Park Road, Tilehouse Street, Bucklersbury, Market Place, Bancroft, Nightingale Road, Walsworth Road, Queen Street, Bridge Street and Sun Street back to Market Place, where it arrived at 8.30 p.m. 'There Captain Delme-Radcliffe, accompanied by Mrs Delme-Radcliffe, made a brief but felicitous speech to the crowd.' (*Hertfordshire Express*.)

In Tilehouse Street the procession was more clearly defined, though oddly caparisoned. 'A lorry-loadful of small Red Cross nurses, with small sick and wounded patients to match . . . there was a load of Japanese geisha . . . Peace, on her warlike charger . . . a couple of waggon-loads of happy lads in khaki and girls in smiles, a brave and earnest contingent of Boy Scouts (striding like giants), and a band of school-children completed the procession.' (*Hertfordshire Express.*)

The 'Peace' float from the procession, on Butts Close.

Peace brought the realization that such slaughter should never happen again, and war memorials sprang up all around the country. Hitchin's was dedicated on 6 August 1922. As the space around the memorial itself was limited, the service of dedication was held in Market Place – from the back of a lorry draped with the Union flag. The service was led by the vicar, the Revd L.B. Ashby, and the Minister of the Tilehouse Street Baptist church, the Revd J. McCleery, accompanied by the Lord Lieutenant of Hertfordshire, Viscount Hampden.

The weather that day was appropriately sombre, and after the service had taken place the townspeople were invited to process past the new memorial in fours. 'It was a little to be regretted that the actual unveiling could not be seen by the greater part of the Market Place assembly . . . Lord Hampden, accompanied by the platform party, walked to the memorial. He cut a cord, and the canvas sheeting and the two Union Jacks masking the front of the memorial fell apart.' (*Luton News.*)

In 1929 a major extension to the North Herts. and South Beds. Infirmary was completed. The new block was opened by the Duchess of York and part of the celebrations comprised a procession, which is seen here coming down Hermitage Road. In the foreground are representatives of the St John Ambulance Brigade.

The Duchess drove from the Infirmary to the Priory; many people had gathered in Brand Street to watch her pass.

At the Priory further speeches were made to the assembled company, and as well as performing the official opening of the extension, the Duchess of York presented long-service decorations to members of the St John Ambulance Brigade.

The modifications to the Infirmary included a new main ward, two new private wards, the combination of two older wards to make a new larger one, and residential accommodation for nursing staff. This view was taken shortly before the clearance of the whole Lairage site in 1988.

Mr A. Cook received first prize in the Hospital Procession (Horse-Drawn Vehicles Class) for the 'Hospital Helps All Classes' float, seen here at the junction of Bridge Street and Tilehouse Street.

The celebrations for the coronation of George VI in 1937 were naturally marked by processions through the town. The one seen here is at the southern end of the High Street.

Putting up decorations for the 1937 coronation celebrations outside Cannon's fruiterer's shop in the High Street. There was a 21-gun salute in Priory Park, a carnival at Top Field with an athletics display by Grammar School boys, a fun-fair on Butts Close, and an old folks' tea in the Town Hall. It was planned to hold evening events on the new St Mary's Square, but it rained hard and the events were postponed. A large crowd did gather there, however, to hear the King's speech broadcast over loudspeakers which had been installed.

The Hermitage Cinema was constructed in 1939. Costing £120,000, it was built to the design of Edgar Simmons, a Letchworth architect, by John Ray Ltd. Tickets for the evening performances ranged from 6d. to 2s. 6d., and could be booked in advance by telephone for an additional 3d.

Air-raid shelters being dug at St Mary's Square, 1939. It is easy to forget that the Second World War did not start instantaneously; there was a long period of tension beforehand. Air Raid Precautions were considered in 1938 and earlier, in light of the effect of bombing in the Spanish Civil War. So, not long after its construction, St Mary's Square was being dug again up to provide these shelters.

Call-up was soon introduced, and these young men give their particulars to the man behind the desk, probably in the Old Town Hall in Brand Street, in 1939. The poster on the left advertises the presence of a public shelter in the Cattle Market, Payne's Park.

The Lairage shelter was indeed substantial, and can be seen here under construction in October 1939. The large building at the right is the end of one of the maternity wards of the Infirmary.

Some people hadn't trusted Hitler in the first place; nor had they believed Neville Chamberlain's cry of 'Peace in our time!' Though this photograph appeared in the *Pictorial* in August 1939, the builder of this fine shelter had dated his work over the lintel 'Built March 28th 1939'.

Evacuees arrived in Hitchin almost immediately after the declaration of war. This young mum arrived by train as part of a large contingent on 5 September 1939, complete with her gas mask in the little cardboard box slung over her shoulder.

With the evacuees came substantial emergency rations, but Hitchin's immediate response seems not to have been one of delight – each evacuee was given only a cup of water on arrival. Here rations of bully-beef are laid out ready for collection in the station yard.

There was a sudden flurry of weddings in 1939; at least the shops still had clothes for the brides to choose from. Many later brides were married in dresses made of old parachute silk. This couple, about to be pelted with confetti, stand outside the sandbagged Register Office, which at that time was in offices above Lloyds Bank. On the wall to the left of the groom, a poster advertises black-out precautions.

Black-out meant more than not showing a light at home; there were no street lights, and special shades were fitted to car headlights. This meant travel at night was extremely hazardous, but stripes were painted on lamp-posts and kerbs to aid visibility.

War strategists claimed that 'the bomber will always get through', and all raids, particularly incendiary raids, were taken seriously. Emergency water supplies, such as these portable water dams photographed in 1939, were being installed in the Lairage. An enormous static water tank was built in the northern half of Market Place (see p. 99).

(see p. 99)

The construction of the water tank forced the market out of Market Place, and by October 1939 it was settling down in its new home on St Mary's Square.

Once war was declared in September 1939, pillboxes sprang up everywhere to challenge the invader. This one, outside Bowman's Mill by the railway station, sported a humorous hoarding. In front stands a gas-detector plate on a stand. On the other side of the railway bridge there was a Home Guard spigot-mortar, rotatable around a steel pin set in a concrete pillar and fired by men in a ring trench around the cylinder.

Other pillbox sites were here in Payne's Park at the junction with Old Park Road, at the junction of St John's Road and Whitehill Road, in Grove Road on the north-eastern side of the railway bridge, and by the bridge over the Purwell in Cambridge Road.

A couple of ARP wardens enjoy a game of darts in Woolgrove Road, Walsworth, 1939. Sandbags soon became a familiar part of the landscape, but the low initial pace of the war in England meant that Civil Defence and ARP staff had little to do, though this was soon to change.

Up went 'Moaning Minnie', the air-raid siren, in January 1940, near to The Biggin. A long, single note denoted 'All Clear', while a slow, sickening yodel meant 'Enemy Approaching'.

A Remembrance Day parade in 1944 passes a large water tank constructed in Market Place to serve as a source of supply for the fire brigade during bombing. The side bears the motif of an S over a wavy line over a W, for Static Water, and there were directions throughout the town to the nearest supply. A motif like this still remains on the wall at Starlings Bridge roundabout, opposite N & P Windows.

A military display in Market Place, 1941. The usual gaggle of boys gather to speculate on how well the troops are doing, while some girls hang out of the window of Timothy White's to get a superior view. The small sign on the pilaster of the Corn Exchange next door proclaims that it is a British Restaurant, where good meals could be had for reasonable prices.

A military display on Butts Close, 18 May 1943. The very open nature of Butts Close at this time makes the identification of landmarks a little difficult. The camouflaged building left of centre is the stand on the football ground, while on the right-hand side is the path across to Fishponds Road, with the swimming pool just out of the picture, top right. The avenue of sweet chestnut trees is only six years old, planted to mark the coronation of George VI.

The Forces' Sweetheart Vera Lynn visits 'a local hospital' in December 1943. The popular star sang for the assembled company, and signed autographs. It is likely that it was Hitchin Hospital, as this was used particularly for military personnel.

Housewives queue for cherries in Bancroft, June 1944. Rationing ensured that while no one had enough food, everyone had some. The more exotic fruits were unobtainable – oranges and bananas, for example – while those which were grown in this country disappeared rapidly once they came into season.

A large bonfire was lit in St Mary's Square in 1945 as the King finished his VJ-Day speech, and dancing, singing, and street parties immediately got under way. During the war in Europe 7,032 bombs fell on the 125 square miles of the Rural District, of which 466 were high explosive and 6,528 were incendiaries. As well as that, 8 parachute mines, 11 flying bombs (V1s) and 4 V2 rockets exploded in the area.

To mark the Festival of Britain in 1951 an immense pageant was held in Priory Park. To say it had a cast of thousands was surely an understatement if this photograph, taken from the control tower over the audience stands, is anything to go by.

Her Majesty the Queen arrives with Viscount Hampden and is greeted by the Festival Maid, Isobel Harkness.

A scene from the pageant itself: the arrival of the Great Northern Railway at Hitchin in 1850. The locomotive was a reproduction of the first one to arrive at Hitchin.

The dress rehearsal took place in front of an audience of 1,600 schoolchildren.

King George VI died in February 1952 at Sandringham, and his body was taken back to London by a train which passed through Hitchin. Many people turned out to watch the train pass through.

The proclamation of Queen Elizabeth II on the steps of the New Town Hall, 1952.

The crowd which greeted the proclamation was markedly smaller than that which rejoiced in the accession of George V in 1911, filling only the upper part of Brand Street down as far as the Dog pub on the left.

One minute's silence was observed for the late King on the occasion of his burial the following week. When the church bell sounded in a curiously deserted Bancroft, pedestrians stood quietly in shop doorways or wherever they happened to be, and cyclists and other traffic stopped at the kerb as a mark of respect.

A scene from the pageant presented at The Dell, Woodside, as part of the celebrations for the coronation of Queen Elizabeth II, 1953. Daphne Guyton was cast as Queen Elizabeth. Although less elaborate than on previous similar occasions, activities still included the election of 'Miss Hitchin', services for schoolchildren, a coronation procession, a coronation bowls competition, a business premises display competition, a coronation service, a distribution of souvenir tea-caddies to housebound people over sixty-five, as well as fancy-dress competitions, square dancing in St Mary's Square, and a firework display.

A scene from the Coronation Pageant, 1953. The Dell had been established as an open-air theatre as part of the general tidying up of Windmill Hill. It was an ideal venue for such events as pageants, though the 1951 Festival of Britain event was on far too large a scale for The Dell. Today the vegetation has advanced somewhat – to the delight of some, and the dismay of others.

The market stalls were never to move back into Market Place after the war. In October 1960, when this photograph was taken, the market was still held in St Mary's Square, and Market Place had a new job as a car park with the cars laid out in a double row on either side of the diagonal route across, just visible in the top right corner. Cottages still ran along Biggin Lane, and St Mary's School still stood. The following decade, however, was to see vast changes throughout the town.

Oakfield Estate in a view looking eastwards, 1960. Built to the south of the town this substantial new estate grew up by the Ash Brook, on what had until 1960 been open agricultural land.

H.A. Saunders & Co., a new temple to the motor car, was erected at the south end of Queen Street in 1963. Only recently (1994) has it changed status, to become a supermarket, restoring shopping activity to this corner of the town centre.

During the sixties there were more serious losses than gains. Perks & Llewellyn's, pharmacists and lavender distillers, ceased trading in 1964. The business had begun in 1790, and from 1823 had specialized in the production of lavender products – washing and shaving soaps, toilet water, dentifrice, even lavender toothpaste. 'The Series of Lavender Bloom Shaving & Toilet Soaps sent out by Messrs Perks are in truth really unique . . . immeasurably superior to any others we have tested.' (*War Office Times and Naval Review*, 1907.)

The new Woolworths shop, which opened for business on 19 August 1965. Perks was replaced by this store, which tried hard to be architecturally sympathetic to its neighbours. Although perhaps exaggerating the features of its predecessor, especially the first floor windows, it has withstood the test of time. The ground floor entrance has been remodelled since its opening.

In 1963 a small and unobtrusive building in Bancroft, a medieval hall-house, became a particularly sad victim of circumstances. Quite dwarfed by the 1924 development next door to it, the hall-house had never found a modern function once it had ceased to be a private house. After short spells as a radio shop and bus offices it was demolished. This photograph was taken around 1930.

North of the town there was a radical change to the skyline as a new industrial complex took shape, shown here in 1964. A Woodhall-Duckham catalytic rich gas plant converted crude naphtha delivered by train to a gas which could be used in ordinary domestic fires and cookers. It could convert up to 30 million cubic feet of gas per day.

Spurrs's had been in the Market-place for nearly a century, but times were changing. The public did not seem as keen on small department stores as on large ones, though they were keen enough to snap up bargains at the July sales here in 1960. By 1965 Spurrs's had been taken over by the Welwyn Department Store, and soon the site was to form the frontage of the new Market Place development.

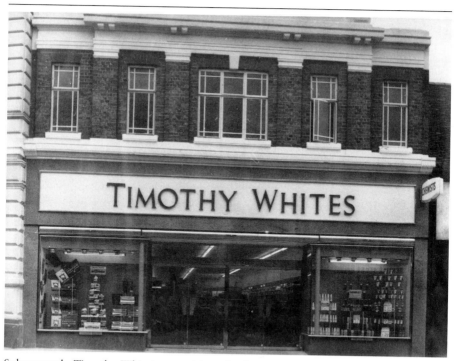

Subsequently Timothy White's moved into the former Woolworths building next to the bank in October 1968.

The space the hall-house had occupied in Bancroft did not remain empty for long, and by April 1967 the whole row up to Portmill Lane had been replaced, by the Co-op on the hall-house site on the left, and a flurry of gable ends to the south.

The gas conversion plant at Cadwell was switched off on 28 October 1974, and thereafter was slowly demolished. The discovery of vast reserves of natural gas under the North Sea made the conversion of naphtha uneconomic.

The Catholic School in Nightingale Road, which had comprised an adaptation of several existing houses, was demolished in 1975.

Late in 1981 the row of cottages which had been joined on to the earlier Waggon and Horses in Old Park Road was demolished to make way for the new bypass.

In 1981 Silverton's, builder's merchants and hardware dealers of Old Park Road, ceased trading, and their building was subsequently demolished. Burr's, the Volvo dealers, expanded to take up the space made available. The building on the left subsequently had its doorway removed and reinserted on the north wall, 90 degrees anticlockwise to the position shown here. Otherwise the building remains substantially unchanged.

While many excellent buildings have vanished, one or two replacements have sprung up that are a cut above the rest. Considering their quality, it is perhaps sad that some of them hide in quiet corners, such as here in Portmill Lane. The neat extension to Hawkins Russell Jones, and the new building on the left, seen here shortly after completion in April 1986, are particularly worthy of comment – imaginative, yet sympathetic to their surroundings.

SECTION NINE

Queen Street

Queen Street from St Mary's church, c. 1905. Just to the right of centre, below the horizon, lies a row of cottages climbing up St Andrew's Place to join Kershaw's Hill. In front of them lies a mass of unplanned tenements, mostly in brick but a few still in timber-frame. Living conditions in these yards were almost indescribable, with large families sharing, in many instances, only two rooms. The river lies at the foot of a line of mature trees which at this stage almost filled the whole churchyard.

Queen Street, c. 1906. The gradual mechanization of agriculture led to a steady displacement of the work-force from the land into the towns. This had gone on throughout the nineteenth century, and Hitchin's story is perhaps unique in detail but typical in outline. Properties fronting Queen Street were to accommodate that work-force, bringing many problems, both social and medical. Many of the houses in the Queen Street area were already very old when this photograph was taken: brick fronts conceal many timber-framed buildings, and gateways on either side reveal later, shoddy structures built hastily to rent out cheaply.

Thorpe's Yard, 1911. Thorpe's Yard was on the eastern side of Queen Street, north of Hollow Lane, and approximately where Garrison Court stands today. This view looks up from the street past houses both of brick and clapboard.

Thorpe's Yard, 1910. Further up the slope, Thorpe's Yard opened out a little. The ground was still covered with coarse stones, and the principal water supply can be seen right of centre, above the bucket. At least there was a piped supply: wells had been the only supply until the early 1850s, and pits the only provision for disposal of human waste – apart from the river. The slow recycling of water from one pit to another led to many outbreaks of cholera.

Sixteen years later, in 1926, the view has not improved: the window, top left, is still open, but more tiles have fallen off the roofs. A figure stands blinking in a doorway, as if to indicate that yes, this is her home.

Chapman's Yard lay on the other side of Queen Street from Thorpe's Yard, and comprised a long row of brick cottages which often housed large families. The other side of the yard was a row of barns. This view was taken between 1910 and 1915.

Barnard's Yard lay just to the north of Biggin Lane and parallel to it. In 1921 the Urban District Council had deemed the area insanitary, but four years later, when this photograph was taken as part of a deliberate photographic record of the area, work was imminent.

St Andrew's Street was no better than anywhere else in the Queen Street area. This view looks west to Queen Street around 1926. In the centre stands the Peahen, and beyond it the Robin Hood, while in Queen Street itself stands the Bushel and Strike. Mr Worbey the window-cleaner lived in the building on the right, while a little further down on the same side lived 'Pompey' French, the bird-scarer. Just out of sight on the left is the entrance to Webb's Yard. Where there was paving, it was not in slabs, but made from grooved engineering bricks.

St Andrew's Place, today a short but precipitous street, in 1910 supported seventeen households in disgusting conditions. The nearer group of cottages appear to be timber-framed, while those further up the slope are of brick. All were demolished in about 1960, and until the construction of the extension to the Telephone Exchange in 1974 the site was a car park.

An aerial view southward of the early phase of the Westmill Estate, 1928/9. The buildings in the centre are The Crescent, with Westmill Road on the left and Mattock Road on the right. Some trees are visible on Butts Close at approximately 10 o'clock.

This view westwards to St Mary's was taken by the *Comet* newspaper's photographer on 29 April 1930. The town was never again to see this level of devastation even during the blitz. The river is invisible behind the trees, and was quite narrow at this point. The inhabitants were rehoused in new council estates in Sunnyside and off Redhill Road.

The changes to Queen Street did not just involve demolition, but included a realignment of St Andrew's Street, and its renaming as Hollow Lane. The site in the right foreground is Garrison Court.

The view from Windmill Hill to St Mary's in 1931. Windmill Hill itself had started to be laid out in the form we know it today. In the foreground is a private garden, and further down is the path which still marks the edge of Windmill Hill and Garrison Court. What is today Portmill Lane car park was still an uncleared site.

A view taken on 14 May 1931, with St Andrew's School on the left and Hollow Lane in the foreground. Some road widening has already taken place.

The same view, taken after the completion of the scheme, with St Andrew's Street metalled. One building, which fronted onto Hollow Lane, has been demolished on the right, and the ground on the eastern side of St Andrew's Street has been laid out as a vegetable plot.

Biggin Lane, *c.* 1926. Warner's Almshouses on Biggin Lane still stand today, but all the surrounding buildings and walls have been cleared, and no record exists of their history or even of their last use.

Other existing facilities had to be relocated, such as Simpson's Almshouses, seen here under construction in Hollow Lane in October 1931.

The whole of Hollow Lane was tidied up: this is the junction with Whitehill Road, the little lane going off to the top right. Whitehill Road was realigned, and presumably it was at this time that the house on the far right was demolished.

Late in 1931 St Mary's Square was virtually complete. The design was Venetian in style, and a text chiselled into the risers of the steps in the central flight (not in the photograph) records the magnitude of the project: '. . . 174 cottages . . . the occupants, 637 in number . . . housed elsewhere A.D. 1925–1929.' Top left stands the Bricklayer's Arms, which also appeared on p. 116; it had been rebuilt in 1922.

Looking south over the roofs of warehouses in Portmill Lane in November 1931, it is clear that much remained to be done on the west side of Queen Street. There were still many cottages in the yards parallel to Biggin Lane, the bulk of which were finally compulsorily purchased in the 1960s.

While the yards off Queen Street may have been cramped and unhygienic, social life flourished. Everyone knew everyone else, and while it may have been true that the policemen only went there in twos, there was a general camaraderie. Many of the women worked at the Sanitary Steam Laundry, and here, just outside it, a substantial party awaits a coach to take them to the British Empire Exhibition at Wembley in 1924. The manageress, Mrs Hyran, sits at the front, and her husband stands, hatted, at the back.

For the men, social life meant the fellowship of the tavern. This is the billiard room of the Peacock, around 1915 – pub interior photographs of this date are not common. The Peacock was taken over by the Herts. and Essex Public House Trust in 1906, to be modernized. Managers there received commission on the sales of non-alcoholic drinks and food, but not on alcohol: until that time the pub had brewed its own beer. In 1927 the Council bought the pub from the House Trust, and carried on trading until the end of 1928. It was then demolished as part of the overall Queen Street scheme.

For the children there was little provision beyond the traditional fairs, occasional circuses and later on the cinema. Some sought to introduce alternatives: in 1915 Aillie Latchmore established a Girls' Club in Queen Street. After 1926 it met regularly in a large hut beside St John's Road, then called Bethel Lane. Here on its opening day in 1926 members stand outside the hut. Viscountess Cecil is in the centre with the bouquet, Aillie Latchmore to the right, and Miss Valentine to the left.

Another view taken from the tower of St Mary's church in 1974 shows clearly the changes that have taken place: new flats fronting the street on the left, Windmill Hill a public park, Hollow Lane and the mighty River Hiz actually visible, noisome slums gone.